Original title:
Overheard in the Overstory

Copyright © 2025 Creative Arts Management OÜ
All rights reserved.

Author: Seraphina Caldwell
ISBN HARDBACK: 978-1-80567-419-1
ISBN PAPERBACK: 978-1-80567-718-5

Lullabies on the Wind

Whispers tickle trees at night,
Squirrels sing, oh what a sight!
Crickets join the serenade,
While sleepy owls serenely fade.

Branches sway in gentle dance,
Silly shadows start to prance.
A lullaby of rustling leaves,
Sings of dreams and midnight thieves.

The Enchanted Grove

In the grove, a leaf took flight,
Caterpillars dance with delight.
The sunbeams giggle on the ground,
As willow whispers secrets found.

Mushrooms wear their little hats,
While raccoons chat with the bats.
A bunny hops and makes a scene,
With twinkling eyes, so bright and keen.

Soliloquies Under the Stars

Stars are gossiping up high,
Moonlit winks and twinkling sighs.
Nights are filled with chatter sweet,
Where crickets and frogs have a meet.

The owls debate the best wise lore,
While fireflies flash like never before.
Each twinkling light, a funny story,
As dreams take wing in golden glory.

Sounds of the Swaying Ferns

Ferns are giggling in the breeze,
Tickled by the playful trees.
Grasshoppers leap with jolly cheer,
They croon their tunes for all to hear.

In a whirl of greens and light,
Laughter echoes into the night.
Nature's choir, oh what a show,
With hums and drums from below.

Whispers of the Canopy

The squirrels gossip loud, quite proud,
Chattering about who's in the crowd.
The birds roll their eyes at the tree's tall show,
'Who wears the best bark? It's a real tree glow!'

The windy whispers tickle the leaves,
'Can you believe it? She finally weaves!
A nest made of twigs and a dash of flair,
Look out, Martha! That's a real fashion dare!'

Beneath the Silent Boughs

The shadows dance and the critters prance,
Mice whisper secrets of their brave romance.
'To nibble or not to nibble, that's the question,'
Squeaked one brave mouse in a queasy confession.

The owls laugh hard at the silly display,
'Who knew romance came in such a cliche?
Kissing in the moonlight, what a cliché spree,
Watch out for cats, or it's history!'

Tales from the Twisted Roots

The roots of the trees host a comedy show,
Where fungi tell jokes, and the earthworms glow.
A toad hopped by, saying, 'What's the punchline?'
The mushrooms erupted, 'I'll tell you—it's fine!'

Underneath the tangled branches galore,
A squirrel made puns, always wanting more.
'I'm nutty for laughter, I just can't stop!'
The trees chuckled back, 'You're the cream of the crop!'

Secrets of the Leafy Kingdom

In the leafy kingdom, a party was set,
Where vines stretched out to see who would bet.
A hedgehog whispered, 'I'm the dance champ here!'
While crickets provided the tunes that we hear.

The ants brought snacks on a leaf-shaped plate,
'You won't believe this! They're really first-rate!'
But a gust of wind knocked the snacks in the air,
And all the tree folk just sighed in despair.

Conversations in the Canopy

Squirrels chattered, bold and brash,
'That nut was mine, you took it, smash!'
Birds sang gossip, high in the trees,
'Think they'll see my new nest? Oh please!'

Monkeys swung, with laughs so sweet,
'I'll steal your cheese, now isn't that neat?'
A frog croaked loud, with a wink,
'Have you seen the owls? They're on the brink!'

Leaves rustled, whispers to share,
'The wind said something, but I don't care!'
The whole forest laughed, a raucous cheer,
Nature's own stand-up, loud and clear!

Shadows of the Ancient Grove

Two acorns plotted, quite a scheme,
'We'll start a band, create a dream!'
A deer joked, 'With you two, I'll pass,
Maybe I'll dance instead on the grass!'

A wise old owl, perched with pride,
'I'm a night owl, come join the ride!'
But raccoons giggled, stealing the show,
'We know the secrets of the glow!'

Branches bending, tales unfold,
Of creatures clever, brave, and bold.
With shadows dancing, laughter flows,
In the ancient grove, anything goes!

Echoes of the Woodland

A rabbit whispered to a squirrel,
'Your tail's getting fluffier, oh what a whirl!'
The squirrel grinned, flicked it just so,
'Standing out's easy when you're this pro!'

Crickets chirped a rhythmic tune,
'You know, I'm thinking we should croon!'
The fireflies blinked with a soft glow,
'Sure, but can you keep time? I don't know!'

Mice gathered, sharing a slice,
'Next week, let's have ice cream, sounds nice!'
In whispers, echoes, laughter, delight,
Woodland stories sparkle under night.

Murmurs of Bark and Leaf

The trees argued, who was the tallest,
'I'm the oldest!' said the stoutest.
Leaves giggled, rustling in play,
'We just blow in the breeze every day!'

A beetle bragged, with a tiny cheer,
'You think you're tall? I'm the fastest here!'
A spider wove tales of her grand web,
'You'll be caught, but don't be a drab!'

Bark heard secrets, whispers implored,
'What's a tree's favorite game? Board!'
All nature laughed, embracing the fun,
In this leafy world, joy's never done!

Songs of the Swaying Elders

In the breeze, they twist and shout,
Old branches gossip, there's no doubt.
Leaves laugh lightly, rustle with glee,
Each whisper shared, a grand jubilee.

Oh, the tales of squirrels and their bravado,
Fluffy-tailed bandits, wielding a nacho!
They spy on the world from their leafy throne,
Conspiring with crows on the wisdom they've sown.

Chatter Beneath the Boughs

The acorns converse, oh what a scene,
Plotting the downfall of the coming green!
"Take that sunshine!" they chirp with delight,
As shadows march in to join the fight.

Frisky raccoons in masks and tuxedos,
Debate whether midnight is their speedo.
With paws on hips and eyes all aglow,
They plan their next raid on the farmer below.

Rustling Secrets in the Underbrush

Frogs hold court in puddles, so round,
Ribbiting news of the latest sound.
"Did you see that bug?" one whispers with glee,
"It had six legs and a flair for the spree!"

Butterflies flit, on a fashion crusade,
Comparing their colors in the sunshade.
"Last season's stripes? Oh, what a bore!"
As they flap their wings, fashion's the score!

The Council of Canopies

Gathered aloft in a woodsy debate,
Branches convene to decide their fate.
"We need a theme for the forest gala,
How about 'Leaves'?" one shouts like a baller."

"Or perhaps 'Bark Fashion'," another insists,
"Inspired by nature's most stylish twists!"
The shadows chuckle, their laughter cascades,
While the sun dips low, afire in parades.

Tales Tucked Among the Twigs

A squirrel wearing a tiny hat,
Scolded a bird for being too fat.
"Stealing my nuts? It's quite a shame!"
"Hurry up! There's no time for blame!"

The tree bark giggled at their fuss,
As a raccoon joined in, quite nonplussed.
"You ought to share, not cause a scene!"
"Who needs to share, when there's so much green?"

A whisper floated up from the ground,
"Why are they yelling? Can't they be found?"
Roots wriggled in laughter, how silly it seemed,
While the branches above just nodded and dreamed.

And so the forest shared tales of delight,
Of squabbles and antics that lasted all night.
In the heart of the woods, they'd just laugh and play,
As nature's own sitcom unfolded each day.

Whispers of the Winding Roots

Down below, where the roots tend to twine,
A worm started chatting with a sprout of pine.
"You think you'll grow big, standing so tall?"
"Just wait and see, I might be the wall!"

A ladybug giggled at their chatter,
"You think that's important? Oh, what a matter!"
"I'll fly around, while you sit and pine,"
"At least my friends think I'm simply divine!"

A mushroom chimed in, feeling quite brave,
"What's so great about a barky old wave?"
"We laugh at the clouds, who drip and who cry,"
"Meanwhile, we root where the fun's on the sly!"

And though the roots tangled beneath the ground,
The laughter above was the funniest sound.
Together they whispered each silly reprieve,
In concert of joy, the forest believed.

Echoes of the Elderwood

In the elderwood, where shadows reside,
An owl who was wise just couldn't abide.
"You thief of my branches, you naughty old crow!"
"My flying skills are better, just thought you should know!"

The fox nearby snickered under his breath,
"Wise owls don't squabble, it's close to your death!"
"Don't tell me to hush, I've got tales to tweet,"
"Of feathery foes and my favorite treats!"

The trees, they all whispered and swayed to the beat,
While a beetle danced sportily, quick on his feet.
"Let's make up a story, a charm of our own,"
"A musical tale of our elderwood throne!"

And so they sang softly, the sounds intertwined,
Echoing giggles of a voluminous kind.
In the heart of the forest, where laughter was bright,
Even wise old owls found joy in the night.

Harmony Among the Hushed Leaves

Leaves rustled softly, sharing a joke,
While a chipmunk sat, playing the bloke.
"What did one leaf say to another so green?"
"We're all in this together – let's go, the unseen!"

Caterpillars laughed at their dance through the air,
"Have you heard the buzz? It's rare but quite fair!"
"Butterflies dreaming can dance all around,"
"But we'll chew our way through, all morning abound!"

The sun peeked in with a bright, cheeky grin,
While the shadows below let the mishaps begin.
"Who tripped on the roots? Oh, what a fine fall!"
"It was I, the proudest! Sorry, and crawl!"

In the boughs above, harmony bloomed,
As every creature shared laughter in tune.
Together they reveled in nature's own play,
Creating a joy that would never decay.

Stories of the Shaded Sanctuary

In the glade, the squirrels chatter,
Over stolen acorns, they scatter.
A raccoon claims he saw a ghost,
But all that's here is his brunch toast.

The owls hoot jokes, all wise and grand,
Sharing tales that are quite unplanned.
The rabbits giggle, tails a-flick,
Laughing at a snail's slow trick.

The chipmunks dance, beneath the leaves,
While ants conspire, plotting their thieves.
The trees listen, their boughs sway,
As nature's comedy steals the day.

So in this realm where whispers play,
And laughter echoes, come what may,
Each shadow sings a funny tune,
Beneath the sun, beneath the moon.

Rumblings of the Roots

Deep below, the worms do squirm,
Sharing secrets, they excel in term.
A toad asks what the groundhog said,
But the grapevine spins tales instead.

The roots do tickle with gossip's tease,
While fungi laugh, at the passing breeze.
The beetles argue over the best route,
And fireflies flash, as if to shout.

A whisper of mud spills a grand affair,
Of moles who think they're the best at dare.
The stones keep quiet, they just roll,
While roots entwine in a goofy stroll.

So down below, where no one sees,
Laughter explodes with such sweet ease,
The earthy tales, from roots so deep,
Keep nature's humor, a thrilling sweep.

Whispers Beneath the Canopy

High above, the leaves share lore,
As squirrels mock the birds, oh what a bore!
A crow caws back, with sass and flair,
"I'm the best at taunting, none can compare!"

The breeze chuckles, weaving through trees,
While crickets chirp up, in harmonic tease.
The foxes roll, critters in delight,
Playing tag under the soft moonlight.

Each branch holds secrets, funny and bright,
Gossipy thieves plotting through the night.
The roots giggle each passing tale,
With every jest, the laughter won't fail.

In this forest of whimsy and play,
Every creature has something to say,
So listen close when you wander through,
For nature's jokes can come right at you.

Secrets Among the Roots

Within the soil, the secrets dwell,
Where beetles plot and whisper well.
A grumpy old gopher checks his watch,
Claiming he's in a mighty botch.

The moles hold court, and jest they posit,
Declaring their digging is rather closet.
A stinging tale of a lost lost sock,
Had roots laughing till they nearly rocked.

Underfoot, where shadows play,
Ants gossip about what the ladybugs say.
"Did you see that?" a twig did crack,
As laughter sprang from every crack.

In the corners where dark things hide,
Echoes of chuckles and joy abide,
For every whisper, a chuckle too,
In the world's great comedy breakthrough.

The Silent Council of Pines

In the canopy, a whisper flows,
Pines gossiping where nobody goes.
"Did you see that squirrel? Quite the show!"
"I hope he doesn't get too close, you know!"

They huddle tight, their needles bend,
Sharing tales of feathered friends.
"Last week, a bluejay told a lie,
He sang so loud, the sun got shy!"

"Remember that time with the windy whoosh?"
Laughter echoed in the leafy bush.
"A branch got tangled, poor fellow fell,
Now he hums a tune in the chipmunk's cell!"

So next time you stroll in the green below,
Listen close to the pine tree show.
With a chuckle and a rustle, they blend their lore,
A comedy club where nature's the core!

Treetop Confessions

Up high, the branches share their truths,
A squirrel admits he's lost his youth.
"Too many nuts and not enough leaps,
I trip over roots while everybody sleeps!"

The owls roll eyes at the sparrow's brag,
"You call that a song? It's more of a wag!"
The sparrow fluffs up, takes a big stance,
"At least I get chickadees to dance!"

A raccoon drops by with a wink and a paw,
"Heard you all laughing; I'm here for the jaw!"
With snacks in tow, he brightens the night,
"Tell me your secrets, I'll keep them tight!"

The treetops tremble with giggles and grins,
A lot can unfold in the world's tall spins.
So next time you wander beneath the sky's lace,
Remember the fun in the greenest place!

Nature's Hidden Narratives

In the shadows, tales intertwine,
Beneath the bark, secrets align.
A bramble boasts, "I'm quite the catch,
I've got wounds and stories, but none to match!"

A ladybug interrupts, with spots in a flurry,
"Your troubles are cute, but I'm in a hurry!"
"I'm off to inspect the neighbor's new bloom,
Heard it's so bright, it clears out the gloom!"

A buzzing bee joins, spreading the buzz,
"Let's join forces; we'll create quite a fuzz!"
Nature's characters, quirky and spry,
Sharing their tales under the vast sky.

So, if you wander where the wild things play,
Listen in closely, there's humor in sway.
For every rustle is a line in the script,
Of nature's own comedy, perfectly flipped!

Passages of the Gnarled Old Wood

The gnarled oak grumbles, feeling quite wise,
"In my many years, I've seen some surprise!"
Whispers of winds make the branches shake,
"You wouldn't believe what these tree trunks take!"

A beetle squeaks, "I'm here for the wood,
I polish and shine, it's all understood!"
"But let me tell you, oh the splinters I've met,
Hilarious moments I'll never forget!"

A fox strolls by with a grin in his eyes,
"I've snatched plenty of snacks; let me apprise!"
"That last acorn? Quite a tough nut!
Had me flipping and flopping, oh what a rut!"

The old wood chuckles with a creak and a groan,
Each passage a tale like a well-spun stone.
So listen closely, all dear aspiring jesters,
For wisdom and laughter come from these testers!

Echoes of the Elderwood

In the forest, squirrels debate,
Who gets the nut on the plate.
A rabbit hops in to say,
"Not all treasure's on display!"

A wise old owl gives a shrug,
"Hey, don't fret, just give a hug!"
The trees sway, whispering glee,
"Life's not just for you and me!"

The raccoons plan their next heist,
"Shiny things are worth the price!"
While foxes argue, loud and brash,
"We prefer a simple stash!"

And as the moon begins to rise,
Frogs start croaking, sharing lies.
Each creature has a tale to tell,
In the woods, all's a show-and-tell!

Conversations Under Starlit Pines

Under pines, the critters chat,
Bears ponder over where they're at.
"Is it June or just a dream?"
"Does anyone care?" the hedgehog beams!

A family of owls hoots in sync,
"Wise or silly? Just what you think?"
A deer joins in, with a grin so wide,
"Why do we talk? Just for the ride!"

Stars twinkle, listening close,
As raccoons argue, just like most.
"Who stole my snack? Was it you?"
"Nope! Blame the bird, it's always true!"

The laughter hangs, like silvery dew,
In nature's circle, it feels so new.
Next time you wander, stop for a while,
Join the chat, share a smile!

The Wordless Chorus of Nature

In the woods, a silence reigns,
Yet whispers float like playful trains.
Breezes swirl with secret spells,
Nature sings, though none can tell.

A frog performs without a care,
While crickets chirp, a nighttime flare.
"Is that a joke?" asks a curious snail,
"Or just a riddle in nature's tale?"

Leaves chuckle as they flutter down,
While branches sport a leafy crown.
Beetles boast of their grand feats,
"I can flip, roll, and then retreat!"

And there, beneath an ancient oak,
The wind tells stories, never spoke.
With chuckles and chuckles, they conspire,
In this lively world, no one tires!

The Hidden Symphony of Roots

Deep below, the roots convene,
Rooted best friends, a leafy scene.
They gossip low beneath the ground,
"Have you seen what grows in town?"

Worms wiggle, chiming in with flair,
"Did you hear the tree's new hair?"
Mushrooms chuckle, sprouting wide,
"We're the stars of this hidden ride!"

A dance of fungi, quite absurd,
"We're trending now! Have you heard?"
The soil jokes, quite full of mirth,
"We keep secrets, that's our worth!"

So next time you stroll above,
Remember the roots and their playful love.
They laugh and sing, under the ground,
In the hidden tunes, joy is found!

The Lament of the Lost Leaves

Oh, the breeze has whisked them away,
Those poor leaves, they just want to stay.
Caught in the whirl of a tree's wild dance,
Now they're off on a leaf-swapping chance.

They whisper of paths through sunlit air,
But land in a yard without a care.
Bawling and drifting, they miss the green,
Now stuck with a dog, their new routine!

Conversations Beneath the Canopy

Hey there, acorn, how's it feel?
A nutty life, with such a great deal?
Just sitting around, waiting to grow,
While squirrels plot schemes for your grand show!

A branch chimed in, "You lot are all nuts!"
"I'm bits of wisdom – no ifs or buts!"
Barking back laughter, the winds take flight,
Canopy gossip, from morning to night!

The Collective of the Canopy

In the heights where the sun likes to peek,
The branches hold secrets, a way to speak.
The upper leaves gossip, a rustling spree,
While shadows below sip their herbal tea.

"Did you hear what the pines said last week?"
"Just tall tales of snow, a pretty peak!"
Giggling softly, the ferns join the chat,
Dishing out drama, with a splash of spat!

Voices Trapped in the Grain

In the wood, we've got stories galore,
Like that time we thought we'd knock on the door.
Splinters sent shivers, a forceful push,
Only to find it was just the big bush!

"Echoes of squirrels!" the splinters cried out,
"Can't trust that bark, it's full of doubt!"
So here we sit, in our wooden domain,
Laughs stuck forever in this gentle grain!

The Symphony of Saplings

Tiny trees having a chat,
Gossiping about what's where at.
One claims it saw a squirrel dance,
Waving its tail like a circus prance.

Leaves nodding in a playful tease,
"Who knew trunks could sway with ease?"
Roots are laughing, tangled in jest,
Getting along, never a nest!

With sunlit smiles, they share their dreams,
Of towering heights and wild streams.
Saplings sing in a breezy choir,
Each scheme stretching up higher and higher.

Nature's nursery, a playful show,
Where whispers spread like seeds that grow.
In this green stage, life finds its tune,
Under the watchful eye of the moon.

Fables in the Ferns

Amidst the fronds, a tale's unfurling,
With every gust, the laughter swirling.
One fern claims it saw a deer,
Dressed in pines and shedding cheer.

Another chirps, "What a sight to see!"
"Did they ask for a cup of tea?"
The breeze carries giggles anew,
As they plot a party with a view.

Mushrooms chuckle, joining the fun,
"We'll dance when the day is done!"
While shadows sip on evening light,
Every secret shared feels just right.

Fern fables weave a silly weave,
Nature's comedy, no one can leave.
With roots in laughter, they entwine,
In this leafy world, all is benign.

Whispers of the Woods

In the shelter of trees, voices arise,
Chirping secrets, amusing the skies.
A poplar claims it's the tallest of men,
While a willow just rolls its eyes again.

"Branches like arms!" says an oak with flair,
"Let's wave to the clouds, if they dare!"
The birch, a comedian, quips in rhymes,
"Who needs a hat? I have fine lines!"

Twigs crack with laughter, shadows will sway,
As roots joke about the soil at play.
Each rustle is like a chuckling cheer,
In this green theater, there's no room for fear.

Whispers gather in a giggling crew,
Sharing tales of the skies so blue.
The woods alive, a jester's parade,
With funny stories that never fade.

Chronicles Written in Bark

With a bark, the trees start a tale,
Of mischief and how they'll prevail.
One trunk boasts of a squirrel's pranks,
While another laughs, giving thanks.

Old and wise, they scribble in rings,
Recording the laughter that each tree brings.
"Remember that storm?" one whispers near,
"When we danced so wild without a single fear!"

Branches shake as they share their news,
Of hopping hares in zany shoes.
The woodland folktales grow so bright,
In the symphony of a whimsical night.

Chronicles etched, each joke a mark,
In this forest, no space for the stark.
With every laugh, the stories take flight,
In the cozy embrace of the twilight.

Ballad of the Fallen Leaves

Once a leaf had big dreams, oh so high,
But it slipped from the branch, said goodbye.
It danced with the wind, in a whirl so grand,
Only to land in a child's sticky hand.

That child had a plan, oh what a sight,
To decorate with leaves, all out of fright.
The leaf sighed softly, thinking of trees,
Wondering if it would return with the bees.

As winter approached, the leaf found a friend,
A squirrel who grinned, saying, "Don't bend!"
They laughed at the snowflakes, so fluffy and white,
Together they plotted to fly with delight.

But seasons keep shifting, as they do every year,
The leaf faded quickly, with nothing to cheer.
Yet it chuckled in autumn, as it changed hue,
At least in its fall, it made quite the view!

Chronicle of the Trees' Heartbeat

In a forest where secrets are shared through the bark,
Old trees tell jokes, with a laugh and a spark.
A wise oak remarked, with a creak and a groan,
"You should hear the whispers when no one's alone!"

The birch giggled softly, with her white dress so bright,
"I overheard a stone, claiming he's quite the sight!"
As the wind blew along, laughter echoed in trees,
Nature's chatty heart pulsing as light as a breeze.

Then came a young sapling, eager to fit in,
"What's the best part of surviving the wind?"
The trees all leaned in, their leaves in a flurry,
"Just sway and have fun, no time for a hurry!"

A squirrel chimed in, rolling his eyes,
"We're all just big plants, let's not act so wise!"
And with that, they roared, a glorious sound,
In the heart of the forest, where joy does abound.

Entwined in the Embrace of Earth

Roots tangled together, a social affair,
Whispering secrets without a single care.
"Did you hear the news?" a tulip did say,
"They're planning a rave when the sun's on display!"

Daisies all chuckled, full of pure glee,
"We'll wear our best petals, come dance by the bee!"
With earthworms applauding in the dark soil below,
They planned for an evening, a vibrant glow.

The daisies did twirl, the yellows and whites,
The roots were all jiving, causing quite sights.
"A worm just slipped under, he fell down the line,
And my, what a crunch! That old beetle's divine!"

As night fell upon them, they basked in their mirth,
For even the smallest can celebrate earth.
With quiet giggles, the plants did entwine,
In the embrace of the soil, in their roots, they'll shine.

Gleanings from the Green Depths

In a garden of green, where the weeds like to brawl,
The tomatoes were plotting, they're having a ball.
"Let's roll like the cucumbers, quick on our feet,
And find out who snores when the night is complete!"

Peeking from leaves, a radish put forth,
"You can never out-fun me, for I'm full of worth!"
The lettuce just chuckled; it knew all too well,
That radish was bluffing, a tale hard to tell.

Then came a young carrot, all innocent charm,
"I'll join in your games, but please don't alarm!"
And thus, they all pranced, from seedling to bloom,
With laughter that echoed, illuminating the room.

As night draped the garden, they whispered with glee,
"Who's the jolliest veggie? It's clearly not me!"
But the truth in this tale, with its fun-sparkling sheen,
Is that laughter's the treasure found deep in the green.

The Language of Leaves

Whispers of leaves, when the breeze is just right,
They tell silly secrets, a comedic delight.
A squirrel interrupts, with acorns in tow,
"Did you hear what the bark said? It's all about the show!"

Rustling and chuckling, the ferns can't keep still,
"Did you see that old tree? He's got quite a skill!"
Pine needles giggle, as they scatter about,
"Last week, a branch fell, oh, what a great rout!"

The sun filters down, with a wink and a grin,
The shadows are laughing, where the fun can begin.
"Why did the flower blush?" asks a bold, cheeky twig,
"Because the sun's rays tickled—it danced a small jig!"

Under the canopy, the chatter flows free,
As nature's young jokers define their esprit.
With every soft rustle, there's a gag in the air,
The leaves all agree: humor's beyond compare!

Musings Among the Maple

Beneath the broad branches, humor takes flight,
A maple remarks, "I'm the tallest in sight!"
The nearby oaks chuckle, they know it's a show,
"But we've got the best acorns, so there! Don't you know?"

The sap starts to flow, like stories unheard,
"You wouldn't believe how many times it's been stirred!"
A bird overhears, strutting proudly with flair,
"I only stop by here for the great maple air!"

The wind pipes up, with a teasing old joke,
"What did the tree say to the leaf? 'You're a soak!'"
Maple bursts out laughing, he's bending with glee,
"I'm sap-suckingly happy, can't you see me?"

As the sun dips low, they share tales anew,
Of critters and quips, and who took a wrong view.
Among the sweet maples, where laughter abounds,
Nature's punchlines echo, with joy all around!

Mysteries in the Mossy Shadows

In shadowy glades, where the mushrooms convene,
Strange whispers arise, like a riddle routine.
A hedgehog, quite wise, claims to know all the lore,
"But why did the snail cross the path? I want more!"

The moss sighs a secret, all green and so soft,
"I caught a pine cone flirting—it must be aloft!"
A rabbit pipes in, with a twitch of his ears,
"And I've heard the owl snicker; it's been at least years!"

Twilight's thick veil cloaks the curious band,
"Do you think that the ferns have a rock band planned?"
The shadows just chuckle, in their leafy embrace,
"Don't mind the old willow; he's lost in the space!"

Under this blanket of twilight and dew,
Where wise-cracking critters share musings so true.
These mysteries gathered, their laughter is crowned,
In the mossy green shadows, where joy can be found!

The Forest's Unspoken Tales

Among the tall trees, a chorus does rise,
With tales of old critters, and comical lies.
The elder pine mutters, with a chuckle so deep,
"Remember the rabbit? He couldn't take a leap!"

A fox winks and giggles, his coat gleaming bright,
"I saw him trip over, what a comical sight!"
The badger rolls over, in the grass, full of mirth,
"You think that's a tale? Oh, just wait for its birth!"

The beech tree scratches bark, looking thoughtful and coy,
"Did you hear about the crow with a shiny new toy?"
This chatter blossoms, like flowers in spring,
The forest just hums with the joy that they bring!

As dusk settles softly, and the stars twinkle bright,
These unspoken stories weave laughter in the night.
In the heart of the forest, where whimsy prevails,
Nature's comedians share their funny tales!

The Poetry of the Ponderosa

In a forest where whispers twirl,
A ponderosa points and gives a whirl.
"Tall trees play hide-and-seek with the sun,
I'm stuck here, what's the fun in being so done?"

The squirrels chatter, plotting their heist,
While the branches sway, like they're having a feast.
"Oh look, a bird took my best sandwich today,
Just another tree struggle in a glorious display!"

The sap drips slowly, a gooey retreat,
A sticky reminder of ages discreet.
"Is it a tear, or just my morning dew?
I'd cry over my bark if only you knew!"

With laughter and rustles, stories unfold,
In the Ponderosa, wisdom's retold.
"If only they'd stop with the heavy breeze,
Maybe then I'd sit whole, but that's just a tease!"

Confessions of the Crooked Trunks

In shadows deep, the trunks confide,
With roots so tangled, they can't decide.
"I curve to the left, then lean to the right,
Should I stand tall or just embrace my height?"

A crooked tree sighs with every gust,
"Do I look majestic? I hope I look just!"
Bending to gossip like leaves in a dance,
"Why do they always take a second glance?"

"My friends are all straight, they judge my weird bend,
But I twist and I turn, what's a tree without friends?"
They gossip and giggle, oh what a scene,
Each trunk has a tale, oh, the antics between!"

With laughter that echoes all through the wood,
These crooked confessions would do if they could.
"Let's raise a toast, to being unique!
In this forest of straight lines, we've found our own freak!"

Symphony of the Soughing Trees

A concert of whispers, the trees take the stage,
Their leaves rustle soft like a turn of the page.
"Can you hear that tune? It's my slipstream solo,
Watch out for the squirrel—he's quite the no-show!"

The branches wave slowly, a conductor at play,
With rhythms of nature, they brighten the day.
"I hit a wrong note; oh, what's a tree's hope?
To sway with the winds, or just run down the slope?"

From root to bark, each harmony's found,
While critters join in with a jubilant sound.
"Is that a frog croaking or a missed tree note?
Whatever it is, it keeps us afloat!"

The orchestra grows as dusk starts to creep,
The sounds of the night help the forest to sleep.
"Tomorrow we'll play for the sun, oh so bright,
And laugh at the moon, in its silvery light!"

Sagas Spun by the Swaying Canopy

Up in the canopy, where secrets are spun,
The tales intertwine like a web in the sun.
"Did you hear about Maple? She danced with the breeze,
Fell right on a snail, oh what a tease!"

With leaves like pages, they flutter and sway,
Creating their legends, come join in the play.
"Who scratched that old oak? A love letter or fight?
I swear I saw Willow blushing last night!"

The whispers travel, a legend in bloom,
Each gust of the wind paints the sky with their gloom.
"If I could write novels about all that I see,
I'd tell tales so grand, you'd all laugh with glee!"

So listen up closely, as stories unwind,
From the branches above, to the roots left behind.
"In the forest of laughter, where everyone can,
We weave our own stories, a tree's master plan!"

Echoes Among the Branches

A squirrel discussed its prize,
The best acorn is always a surprise.
The crow cawed with a twist of fate,
"That's not a nut; it's my old mate!"

A rabbit claimed the grass was stale,
While the bees buzzed tales of their grand trail.
The owl hooted, wise with glee,
"You all have never tasted my tea!"

The woodpecker laughed, loud and clear,
"Why complain when the bark is here?"
A fox shared tales of a clever stride,
"I tricked a hiker, and it felt like a ride!"

With giggles echoing through the leaves,
Nature's laughter, a quilt that weaves.
In the shade of branches, they delight,
Giving joy to the cool, breezy night.

Conversations in the Covert

In whispers low, the ferns all talked,
"Did you see the dog that almost walked?"
A ladybug chimed with a tiny cheer,
"I prefer to fly; adventure's near!"

The hedgehogs rolled, in a tumble of play,
"You can't catch me; I'm too spiky today!"
The chipmunk cheered, "Let's have a race!"
"I'll win without leaving my place!"

The trees leaned close, their leaves aflutter,
"What happened to the squirrel's favorite nutter?"
The bees just buzzed with news unplanned,
"Our pollens are in high demand!"

In hollows and shadows, laughter swirled,
As nature's chatter painted the world.

The Language of the Woods

Underbrush rustled with cheeky clues,
"I heard the fox has worn out his shoes!"
A raccoon laughed, looking quite sly,
"That's nothing; he borrowed mine to try!"

The owls exchanged their nightly gossip,
"Who hooted loud? I lost quite the grip!"
A squirrel bragged, higher and proud,
"I'm known for my stunts, just ask the crowd!"

A woodpecker pecked out a tune,
"This is my gig, wish you could croon!"
The mist whispered, twinkling, bright,
"Let's turn this grove into a dance tonight!"

And with every sound, a spark took flight,
The woods were alive, a true delight.

Murmurs Beneath the Moss

Under the moss, secrets were shared,
"Who stole my berry? I'm feeling quite scared!"
The snails just laughed, all slow and sweet,
"Don't fret, dear friend; it's now a treat!"

The mushrooms huddled, all dressed in spots,
"Let's hold a meeting! We're all tied in knots!"
The ferns nodded, all green and wise,
"I hear it's a hit beneath sunny skies!"

A toad croaked loudly, a born entertainer,
"You say you're the best? Well, I'm the not-er!"
The ladybirds giggled, floating away,
"We just want fun; let's all dance and play!"

And so the whispers turned into songs,
Underneath the moss, where everyone belongs.

Chants of the Creaking Branches

The branches groan with tales so tall,
A squirrel's debate on the best nut at all.
Some bark about the winds that sway,
While others gossip of the sun's hot ray.

A robin claims he saw a cat,
In the midst of a lively acorn spat.
The leaves dance in laughter so spry,
Whiskers twitch, oh me, oh my!

Old tree knots tell of barky puffs,
As deer chuckle at the rabbits' bluffs.
In the woods, tales twist and spin,
Nature's humor, a delightful win!

Through noisy woods with antics bold,
The stories shared, never grow old.
From twig to root, it's quite a scene,
Where laughter grows in shades of green.

Secrets in the Underbrush

In the thicket whispers bloom and swell,
Mossy secrets they're eager to tell.
A frog debates his best lily pad,
While shy fox giggles at the old tomcat.

In the shadows, a snail makes haste,
Claiming titles of the slowest race.
Ants march by with tales quite tall,
"Never trust a bug who can't crawl!"

The hedgehogs chuckle, strategy sublime,
Planning their hedgy heists, oh so prime!
Beneath the leaves, they share their dreams,
In this hush, all's not as it seems!

Underbrush life is a comic play,
Odd couples chat, come what may.
With winks of petals and rustles grand,
Secrets thrive, hand in hand.

Lingering Whispers of the Wild

The wind skims past with a cheeky cheer,
It tickles the ferns, "Did you hear?"
A chorus of crickets sing out loud,
Making fun of clouds, whimsical and proud.

A lizard lounges in sun's embrace,
Cracking jokes about the slow-moving space.
"O snail," he jests, "don't take it to heart,
Style's good, but speed's an art!"

Breezes tease the daisies' flair,
In puddles, frogs dance without a care.
"Is it just me or are flies quite thick?"
They croak as they dodge, quick and slick.

The laughter echoes through trees of old,
Nature's humor, a treasure to behold.
In every rustle, a giggle's found,
Where gentle whispers of joy abound.

The Dialogue of Dappled Light

Sunbeams chat as they skip and blend,
Casting shadows that twist and bend.
"Hey there, leaf, lighten up your game!"
The light teases back, "I'll play the same!"

Fluttering wings join the light-hearted fray,
"Got a minute to chat? Let's brighten the day!"
As the flowers nod, their colors bright,
The sun-dappled scene sparkles with delight.

The brook giggles, sharing tales of its flow,
"Just don't rush and forget the show!"
The sunlight winks, "Now that's a wise tip,
Don't splash too hard, or you'll take a dip!"

Together they dance through branches and halls,
Nature's laughter echoes and calls.
In this mixed company, joy takes flight,
Oh, the fun found in dappled light!

The Forest's Hidden Histories

In the woods, leaves gossip, quite the tale,
Trees shake their branches, as squirrels wail.
Mushrooms chuckle under the moonlit gown,
While shadows argue who wears the crown.

The old oak claims to know all the trees,
While vines trail behind, curling with ease.
A beetle boasts of a daring flight,
As whispers float through the starry night.

Birds chirp in codes, a secret club,
Where the owl hoots jokes, served up in a pub.
As rabbits roll dice in a game of chance,
The forest laughs in a spirited dance.

So pause and listen, dear adventurer bold,
For the stories of trees are priceless gold.
When the breeze plays a tune, and branches sway,
You might just hear what the forest will say.

Fables from the Forest

Once a squirrel wore a tiny top hat,
He showed off his moves; it was quite the spat.
With acorns aplenty, he threw quite the spree,
While the chipmunks cheered, "Oh, do come see!"

A pair of foxes held a debate,
About who could run with the most innate fate.
One claimed to be fast, the other was sly,
They raced through the thickets, oh my, oh my!

A raccoon with glasses read tales by the creek,
His friends gathered 'round, not a word did they speak.
With giggles and snorts, they learned to delight,
In fables so funny, by the firelight.

Now when you wander the wild and the green,
Remember the laughter that's often unseen.
For every tree holds a tale of its own,
In this whimsical world, you're never alone.

Sigils in the Sap

Upon the bark, sigils of sap,
Stories etched deep in the tree's tiny map.
A woodpecker knocks out a rhythm so sweet,
While ants march along to a funky beat.

The elder pine tells of weathered woes,
Of storms and winds, and the mischief it knows.
A chipmunk giggles at the tales of the wise,
As dappled sunlight dances through leaves in disguise.

Bees hum a tune as they flit to and fro,
Discussing the best flowers from which they could glow.
With nectar so rich, oh, the gossip they weave,
A honey-dipped melody no one can believe.

Listen for laughter in the rustling leaves,
For the forest's secrets are what it believes.
In the sticky sweet sap, the stories entwined,
With each drop that falls, a new jingle aligned.

Conversations on the Canopy's Edge

At the top of the trees, where eagles reside,
Squirrels debate, and the winds act as guide.
"Did you see the crow?" chirps a young jay,
"He wore a fine coat, oh, hip hip hooray!"

The leaves quiver, gossip shedding their light,
As the sun winks down, turning day into night.
"Let's toast!" chirps a songbird, full of delight,
"Here's to the forest and all its crazy sights!"

A parrot insists he can talk like a clock,
While a wise old turtle just takes stock.
"Time's overrated," says he with a grin,
"Let's just sit here and let the fun begin."

So join in the chatter, don't be shy or meek,
For laughter's the language that nature does speak.
With branches as arms, the forest will sway,
In conversations of joy, come what may!

Chronicles of the Forest Floor

The mushrooms whispered secrets low,
About the deer who put on quite a show.
Squirrels giggled, tails held high,
As they watched a snail that just passed by.

The ants held court on a twig so grand,
Discussing the best crumb in the land.
A beetle rolled in, bragging and bold,
"Mine's the finest—worth its weight in gold!"

Nearby, a hedgehog grinned with glee,
As the fox tried to climb up a tree.
With a thud and a splat, he landed wide,
While the laughter echoed from every side.

Endless tales the forest could share,
Of mischief and pranks, just two to spare.
For beneath the green, life bubbles up,
With stories more punchy than juice in a cup!

Thoughts in the Thicket

In the thicket, thoughts took flight,
A rabbit pondered, day turned to night.
"Is grass really greener?" it asked the hare,
Who just twitched his nose with a skeptical stare.

A wise old owl, perched high and prim,
Hooted, "Life's simple, find joy on a whim!"
But the raccoon just chuckled, a bandit by trade,
"Joy's in the trash!" he happily said.

Beneath the boughs, the chatter was rich,
Joking about a squirrel who lost his niche.
"Did you see him fall? What a sight!"
They laughed and rolled till the moon shone bright.

"Here's to the tales through branches they send,
Let's celebrate nonsense, my silly friends!"
With a swirl of leaves and a touch of cheer,
The thicket sang loud for all to hear.

Voices of the Verdant

In the verdant glade, the gossip spread,
"Did you hear about the bird with a red bed?"
The frogs were croaking, their voices so clear,
Swapping stories with chuckles and cheer.

A caterpillar claimed it would soon transform,
While the flies laughed, "You'll become our swarm!"
Under the sun, the grasshoppers leapt,
Joking about dreams, and secrets well-kept.

The ferns swayed lightly, as if to agree,
While the bushes shook with mirth under the tree.
"Have you tried dancing with no feet?" they cried,
"Let's see you wobble and let laughter guide!"

With whispers of leaves in the gentle breeze,
The verdant voices asked, "Who next will tease?"
Life's just a jest, in this leafy retreat,
More laughs to unearth with every heartbeat!

Gossip of the Great Oaks

Beneath the great oak, the elders convene,
Whispers entwined in a leafy routine.
"Have you seen that crow with a shiny new thing?"
"Such a show-off," the old oak would fling.

"Let's discuss the weather—it's all turned chill,"
Said one grizzled branch, with roots that can't thrill.
But a wind blew by, scattering their fears,
"Let's talk about acorns, and toast with our cheers!"

The squirrels gathered, for tales and for food,
Chomping and laughing in their rambunctious mood.
"Did you taste the nut that fell from the sky?"
A chorus of voices, "Oh, my, oh, my!"

With laughter and stories, the evening took flight,
Underneath canopies, shadowed from light.
The gossip of oaks, a spectacle vast,
In the whispers of woods, their joy will last!

Ponderings of the Perennials

The daisies chat of the sun's bright rays,
While dandelions boast of their wild days.
"A pollen party? Count me in!"
"Oh no, not that again! What a sin!"

The roses giggle, jealous of their height,
"If I could reach you, I'd have quite the sight!"
But the sunflowers just smile with their cheer,
"Take a trip up; we'll all meet here!"

The violets whisper of secret dreams,
Of how to steal the show with their gleams.
"Petals and leaves, such a lovely crowd!"
"But do keep it quiet; don't shout too loud!"

And in the garden under skies so vast,
Both faces of the future and memories past.
Amidst all the laughter, they all agree,
Life's a bloom, so just let it be!

Resonance of the Rooted

Down in the soil, the worms take stage,
"This is our show! Forget the human age!"
They wiggle and dance, making quite a fuss,
While the tree roots muffle, "Can we just discuss?"

"We hold the earth, keep it steady and fine,"
Muttered the oaks, with their old trees' line.
"Yet, who's that croaking by the pond's edge?"
"A frog with a dream, or a mad old hedge!"

The ferns swayed, wise in their way,
"Let them be loud; life's meant to sway!"
As the roots chuckled, entwined and glum,
"With all of this noise, we'd prefer some hum!"

But in the dance of the flora so bright,
Every little sound made pure delight.
A gathering where all souls can be free,
And the earth beneath keeps the giggles in spree!

Stories from the Shade

Beneath the branches, the tales unfold,
Of squirrels and acorns, both brave and bold.
"Did you hear? That oak tried to dance!"
"Oh please, not again! It had no chance!"

The shadows murmured, casting their lore,
As the sun peeked in, looking for more.
"What's that over there? A lost little leaf!"
"Stop mocking it now, the poor thing's in grief!"

A gathering of petals, stories to share,
Of mishaps and blunders without any care.
"The world spins on, let's wrap it in cheer!"
"Or else we'll be stuck here every year!"

And from the shade, they laughed and they played,
Creating a rhythm, a bond unafraid.
For every whisper and rumor would blend,
In the heart of the forest, where giggles transcend!

Echoes from the Elder Trees

The elders swayed, wise in their sway,
Sharing old secrets from long, long ago day.
"Remember that storm when we nearly cracked?"
"Ah, yes! Such a dance; we were quite attacked!"

Their bark is rough, but their spirits are light,
"Let's tell the young ones we ruled the night!"
And the saplings listened, with eyes open wide,
"Did you really make the moon shyly hide?"

The echoes of laughter circled the glade,
With every old tale, fresh memories made.
"Let's sing of the times when we yelled at the sky,"
"And storms called your name! Oh, my, oh my!"

For every root, twist, and calloused embrace,
Brings stories alive, in this magical space.
The laughter of trees is a vibrant spree,
An echoing joy in the lush tapestry!

www.ingramcontent.com/pod-product-compliance
Lightning Source LLC
Chambersburg PA
CBHW071813160426
43209CB00003B/75